THE OFFICIAL PLONKER'S HANDBOOK

CHARLES ALVERSON

Illustrated by David Mostyn

Hippo Books
Scholastic Publications Limited
London

Scholastic Publications Ltd,
10 Earlham Street, London WC2H 9RX, UK

Scholastic Inc,
730 Broadway, New York, NY 10003, USA

Scholastic Tab Publications Ltd,
123 Newkirk Road, Richmond Hill,
Ontario L4C 3G5, Canada

Ashton Scholastic Pty Ltd,
P O Box 579, Gosford, New South Wales,
Australia

Ashton Scholastic Ltd,
165 Marua Road, Panmure, Auckland 6,
New Zealand

Text copyright © Charles Alverson
Illustrations copyright © David Mostyn

First published 1989

ISBN 0 590 76133 1

All rights reserved

Made and printed by Cox & Wyman Ltd,
Reading, Berks
Typeset in Plantin by
AKM Associates (UK) Ltd, Southall, London

10 9 8 7 6 5 4 3 2 1

CONTENTS

INTRODUCTION

by A. Plonker

Welcome to the Official Plonker's Handbook. It's fairly obvious that you're not a Plonker yourself because if you were, you could not have managed to bring together in one place at the same time:

1. Yourself
2. The money required
3. The shop where the Handbook was for sale
4. The sheer ability to give 2. to 3., much less manage the change.

And even if you had, you'd probably have lost the book before leaving the shop. No, *you're* no Plonker. Not you. Never! Then, why buy this book (except, perhaps, to enrich the author, who may or may not be a Plonker himself)?

That's simple. For the same reason that some people buy a copy of, say, *Birds of that Fiddly Little Bit in the Lower Southwest Corner of Eastern Croatia* without actually *being* a scarlet-crested grubwort themselves. Many will want to study the colourful ways of the classic Plonker for the quiet pleasure of spotting one on the street or on the No 37 bus. Others may want to go to a costume party dressed as a Plonker (see page 7 for The Plonker's Wardrobe) or to verify a long-held suspicion that the downstairs neighbour who plays the soundtrack LP from *The Sound of Music* every night from seven pm until two in the morning actually is a genuine Plonker.

Whatever your reason (or even if you're simply a rich person with money to throw away on a specious book about a possibly non-existent human sub-culture), after you've read this book you'll certainly know as much (if not less) than the average person about the Plonkers among us. Forewarned is fore-armed, I always say, though I can't think why and it *does* annoy my pork butcher. But then almost every-thing annoys my pork butcher, especially people who come into his shop and disturb his close examination of Miss Page Three (part of his Open University degree course, he claims) by wittering on about a couple of nice loin chops or a crown roast which must feed seven as Aunt Jessica is coming to lunch this Sunday, and she's an absolute pig.

But – you may well ask – what good will it do to know considerably more about Plonkers than they know about themselves? The answer to that one is simple: I haven't a clue. *You* bought the book, remember. Nobody twisted your arm. Somebody did? Well, I suggest that you change booksellers. That is unless you're the sort of person who *likes* to have their arm twisted by demented booksellers.

On the other hand, this book will be of tremendous value to anyone who should want to *become* a Plonker him(or her)self. In fact, it is absolutely necessary. I

mean, would you set out to become an airline pilot or a brain surgeon without first at least leafing through the appropriate *How to . . .* manual? Of course not. Beware, though, of books which claim that they can teach you how to be *both* an airline pilot and a brain surgeon. Such claims are often exaggerated. You could find yourself shouting: "I said sponge, not forceps, dammit!" at your navigator or mistaking your patient's *hippocampus major* for an in-flight dinner. Which could be embarrassing.

Careful study of this book and patient practice should equip any person of sub-normal intelligence to join the happy ranks of the Plonker. Simply read and memorize a chapter of this book each week and follow its advice and it will not be long before you cannot step outside your door without hearing someone cry: "What a Plonker!"

If for any reason, people already cry this when you step outside your door, tough. It is the policy of this book *not* to make refunds.

We may be Plonkers, but we're not stupid.

1. THE PLONKER'S I.D. CARD

PLONKER IDENTITY CARD

I.M.A. Plonker

This card, should you have any doubts, will identify the bearer as a Plonker. Quite likely, this will be unnecessary as he will probably already have 1. stepped on your toe, 2. spilled soup in your lap, 3. both. Do not be alarmed. He is not dangerous. Just a nuisance.

2. THE PLONKER'S WARDROBE

HAT: A woolly hat with a bobble on it. In the summer, he also wears a woolly hat with a bobble on it. There are some who suspect that his head *also* has a bobble on it.

SPECTACLES: National Health Service with at least one lense cracked and one lense with a pigeon dropping smeared across it.

COLLAR: The bigger and floppier the better.

TIE: Multi-coloured, preferably with big pink and scarlet stripes, at least six inches across at the bottom, and tied with a big fat knot.

SHIRT: Ex-cub Scout (without any badges).

SHIRT POCKET: Bristling with ballpoint pens, none of which actually work.

SHIRT CUFF: Always damp from being accident-ally dipped in something or other.

JUMPER: Tank-top of some indescribable colour, at least two sizes too small.

7

BELT: Latvian war surplus with dangling end at least twelve inches long.

TROUSERS: Maroon sta-prest polyester which glows slightly, especially in the dark. In warm weather, shorts may be worn, but they must be incredibly wrinkled and flop dangerously around upper thighs.

SOCKS: Knee-high, especially with shorts, but fashionable Plonkers usually make sure that the elastic has gone in one sock (the left) so that it sags down to the ankle.

SHOES: Cheap, off-brand trainers usually emblazoned with the name of an animal such as *STOAT*, *WEASEL*, or *LEMUR*.

SCHOOLBAG: Either World War I gas mask case still smelling of mustard gas or imitation vinyl briefcase bought from a petrol station.

3. THE PLONKER'S FAMILY

DAD: An ex-Plonker himself, Dad has grown up to be a fully-fledged nerd, or, if he worked very hard at it, a genuine wally. He is lucky in that his job specifically requires him to be a wally – he's a local radio disc jockey or a market researcher who stands on street corners with a clipboard or a traffic warden or one of the Game for a Laugh team.

MUM: Not a bad sort. Still can't figure out how she managed to end up as both the wife and mother of a Plonker. Does her best to protect Plonker from the consequences of *being* a Plonker, but often finds herself looking forward to the time when he is 18 and will leave home. Doesn't have a clue that he doesn't plan to leave home at all.

OLDER BROTHER: Graduate (well, former student, anyway) of school (Plonker of the Year '86/'87), now on tenth government training programme working as entrails sorter at local slaughterhouse.

SIS: Doesn't actually have a job, but spends all day sitting around the house buffing her nails until the telephone rings. Then has been known to disappear for weeks, and once had to be sent home from an Arab State by the local British Embassy.

UNCLE ERNIE: Just out (again) of the "home", Uncle Ernie makes a habit of coming to the Plonker's school to apply for job of headmaster, teacher, lavatory cleaner. Usually police have to be called to get rid of him.

AUNTIE VI: Famous local shoplifter. Got in the *News of the World* once for trying to sneak three hams, a case of Spanish Champagne and a bag of charcoal brickettes out of Sainsbury's in her bra.

COUSIN ELMO: Apprentice pickpocket. Once attempted to lift wallet of tourist visiting from Paraguay, but got hand stuck. Sends postcards home twice a year, and Plonker collects Paraguayan stamps.

GRAN: Notorious local bag lady. Spends most days on street outside Plonker's school rooting through rubbish bins. Whenever she sees the Plonker in the school yard she hails him and asks him to reach right to the bottom of the bin for something juicy she can't quite reach. Has twice had to be rescued by Fire Brigade from especially deep bin.

GRANDPA: Well-known dirty old man. Spends most days at local newsagents reading tabloid newspapers and calling complete strangers over to admire particular photos. Has been featured in a few headlines in the *Stun* himself: AGEING LECHER IN FISTFIGHT ROW WITH BLIND NEWSAGENT.

4. THE PLONKER'S HOME

NEIGHBOURHOOD: Where they finally located that high-level nuclear waste dump and high-security prison for the criminally insane and violent.

HOUSE: Prefabricated, recycled cardboard underground ranchstyle garden shed.

NEIGHBOURS: On the right: Twenty-four hour serve-yourself wholesale abbatoir with railway spur.

On the left: We-Never-Close Megadecibel disco for deranged headbangers.

Across the street: Combination steel foundry and crematorium.

ROOM: Cupboard under stairs.

BED: An ironing board.

GARDEN: All concrete with asbestos borders. Used as neighbourhood tip. The only plants which will grow turn out to be poison ivy which he mistakes for Chinese lettuce.

DOG: Battersea Dog's Home reject. Rescued from cosmetics manufacturer's laboratory. Suspected of originally being a cat. Will respond only to name of "Kitty".

CAT: Retired circus leopard. Not actually so much retired as fired for eating one too many trainers. Sleeps on the end on Plonker's ironing board and *hates* being disturbed in the morning. Or the afternoon. Not house-trained.

THE FAMILY CAR: 1959 hearse (MOT failure).

BIKE: Army surplus tricycle.

5. THE EVOLUTION OF THE PLONKER

It's hard to believe, but the Plonker and modern man (*homo so-called sapiens*) share many common ancestors. Despite their many obvious differences and the Plonker's uncanny ability to imitate lower life forms, a minor mishap many thousands of years ago (one of the Plonker's earliest forebears married a moss-covered tree branch under the impression that it was the female of the species) resulted in a genetic divergence which has resulted in the vastly different species we see today. The Plonker may speak a similar language as us and eat some of the same foods, though invariably spilling more on his shirt, but as the chart overleaf indicates his claim to be closely related to the human being is somewhat exaggerated.

CHART REPRESENTING THE EVOLUTION
OF THE PLONKER

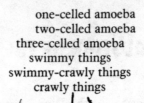

one-celled amoeba
two-celled amoeba
three-celled amoeba
swimmy things
swimmy-crawly things
crawly things

crawly-walky things
slugs
bigger slugs
really big, disgusting
slugs
snails
armadillos
dinosaurs
apes
gorillas
guerrillas
Brook Bond
chimpanzees
cavemen
tree men

crawly things with   terraced house men
3 eyes (became   semi-detached man
extinct for glasses   modern (or detached)
with three lenses)   man

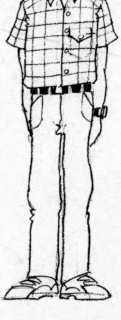

16

crawly things
wearing white socks
fungus
moss
no-parking signs
doorknobs
used-car salesmen
oil slick
whoopee cushions
geography teacher
traffic warden
missing link
disc jockey
game show
presenter
broken link
talk-show host
The Plonker

6. A DAY IN THE LIFE OF A PLONKER

3:30 am: Woken up by Sis coming home from date. Considerable shouting because Mum was woken, too.

7 am: Mum woke me for school.

8 am: Mum woke me for school again.

8:55 am: Mum *really* woke me for school. Very cold. Threw the bucket at me, too.

9:20 am: Late for school again.

10:15 am: Forgot homework for Geography again. Miss Spritt started sobbing and had to be taken to teacher's lounge. Before Mr Twaddle came in to take over class, Simon got me in a headlock and pulled my nose. Mr Twaddle didn't seem to notice at first. Then he did notice and gave me 100 lines.

Noon: Spent lunch hour hiding in toilets. Sent first year with money to bring me some chips for lunch. He didn't come back.

1:07 pm: Late for first afternoon class. Got to Sociology and found no one there. Remembered class was going on trip to local law courts. Ran but arrived to find bus just disappearing. Headmaster asked me if I belonged to school. Didn't seem to believe me.

2:30 pm: Discovered that someone had glued my Chemistry book together. Mr Gass gave me detention.

3:30 pm: School day ends.

3:31 pm: Detention with Mr Gass. He makes me clean thousands of test tubes. Some breakage.

4:45 pm: Released from detention.

4:49 pm: Trapped by Simon in bicycle shed and relieved of 19p, biro, three rubber bands and drawing I made of Donna Lee Snodgrass.

5:10 pm: Arrived home. Threatening phone call from Donna Lee Snodgrass's big (and I mean *big*) brother asking what did I mean drawing nasty pictures of his sister. Says he and his mates will get me.

5:11 pm: Rings back to say that he'll let me off if I'll introduce him to Sis.

5:20 pm: Revise.

5:22 pm: Called by Mum to help her prepare tea. Sis still sleeping.

5:45 pm: Manage to break 3 plates and set frying pan alight.

6:15 pm: Revise.

6:17 pm: Dad asks me to help him clean the ferret cages. In a bad mood after tea breakages. Bitten on thumb by ferret, let 2 escape. Dad does very strange tribal dance.

7:00 pm: Revise.

7:02 pm: Telephone call from police asking will we please come get Uncle Ernie. Say he's been impersonating the Bishop of Stepney – again.

8:20 pm: Back from police station. Uncle Ernie refused to come home, but brought Gran who was found asleep in the bottom of a skip in the Isle of Dogs. Had to carry her three full shopping bags all the way.

8:30 pm: Revise.

8.33 pm: Sis in panic because she overslept. Asks me to paint her toenails while she does her hair. Can't find the turpentine for Sis – she wasn't very pleased with the effects of Dulux Supergloss on her nails.

9:00 pm: Sis leaves in Rolls Royce carrying suitcase.

9:01 pm: Revise.

9:03 pm: Dad comes in with dead ferret. We decide to stuff and mount it. Mum faints when she finds us disembowelling ferret in the sitting room.

9:30 pm: Realize that I have forgotten to bring the correct books home from school. Have been revising from past copies of *Home and Garden* for my Chemistry exam.

10:00 pm: Telly. Grandpa on ITV news for obscene phone calls. From police station while visiting Uncle Ernie.

10:30 pm: Bedtime.

7. THE PLONKER'S NATURAL ENEMIES
(and how they see him)

HEADMASTER: Remote figure who never remembers who the Plonker is even after the Plonker has been at his school for three or four years. Usually greets him with: "I say – er – boy, do you *go* to this school?"

DEPUTY HEAD: Sinister creature who resembles Darth Vader in "Star Wars" but without such a warm personality. Knows Plonker all too well. Has him filed under S for Scapegoat.

HEAD BOY: The head boy does not even recognize that the Plonker is alive except to point him out as a bad example to new students.

SCHOOL BULLY: Probably pays more attention to Plonker than anyone else at school, but since this mostly takes the form of pushing grass up nose, punching and twisting arm, kicking shins, stealing cap, glasses, lunch, etc, this is attention that the Plonker could probably do without.

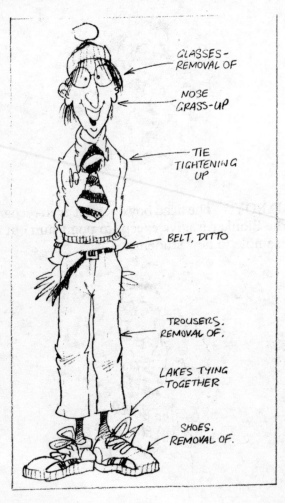

GLASSES - REMOVAL OF

NOSE GRASS-UP

TIE TIGHTENING UP

BELT, DITTO

TROUSERS, REMOVAL OF.

LAKES TYING TOGETHER

SHOES. REMOVAL OF.

CRICKET CAPTAIN: Considers the Plonker as simply an obstruction between himself and wicket-keeper.

LEADER OF THE PACK: Doesn't ordinarily bother with the Plonker except when he comes in handy as a source of small change and a useful shield against lethal missiles.

CAREERS ADVISOR: Will usually try to convince Plonker that the assistant number three man's job (temporary, unpensionable) at the local sewer works is the best job he can hope for.

LOCAL BOBBY: Probably likes the Plonker better than anyone else, mostly because the Plonker comes in handy when he can't find out who did some local crime.

8. THE PLONKER IS THE ONE WHO...

In a crowd, a trained eye can pick out which one is the Plonker. He is the one who . . .

. . . brings the school Christmas Fair to a spectacular early close by accidentally dropping his ferret into the Lucky Dip.

. . . during a fire drill suddenly remembers that he forgot his Mickey Mouse pencil in the Geography room, trips up the headmaster, knocks over the buckets of sand in the main corridor and has to make a jump on to mattresses from a fifth floor window when he realizes that there really *was* a fire.

. . . pulls the train communication cord because he thinks it is the way to order a coke.

... creates panic on the school sports day by getting so carried away in the 50-metre sack race that he forgets that he isn't wearing a belt.

. . . spoils the day trip to France by jokingly telling customs officers that there is a bomb and a kilo of marijuana hidden among the luggage on the school coach.

. . . drops the baton in the inter-school sports relay race, runs back to get it and trips over the rest of the field.

. . . enlivens a visit from the schools' inspectors by choosing that day to throw up all over the lunch table.

. . . dials 999 when he gets the tail of his shirt caught in his flies.

. . . makes all the other kids at the parents' evening feel fortunate when his mother mistakes the school caretaker for the headmaster and his father turns up with his market researcher's clipboard and asks all the teachers what brand of anti-perspirant they use.

. . . greets visiting foreign dignitaries at the school by jabbering at them in his unique brand of German when they happen to be from China, and attempting to rub noses with them.

9. OFFICIAL PLONKER EMERGENCY KIT

A Plonker should never be without the following essential items:

Dirty pocket handkerchief
Extra white socks (extra large, so the toe needs to be folded down)
Extra spectacles (one broken lense, one lense smeared with an indescribable substance)
Street map of Katmandu*
Box of matches (used)
Darts target (inflatable)
Water depurification tablets
Compass (no magnetic needle)
Illuminated sundial (for night use)
Dictionary of Urdu slang**
Anvil
Giant bicycle clips (for wearing with shorts)
Moonlight lotion
79 pence worth of cancelled Sri Lankan postage
Autograph of Princess Michael of Kent
Underwater bird caller
Chewing gum (used)
Instructions for building an igloo

* except for residents of Katmandu
** not available in Urdu-speaking areas

10. THE PLONKER'S CREDO

Follow these five steps, and you will never fail to be a Plonker:

1. NEVER show any taste or discernment.
2. ALWAYS act insensitively towards others.
3. NEVER do anything without messing up.
4. ALWAYS get the blame, especially if you didn't do it.
5. NEVER take your bicycle clips off.

11. THE OFFICIAL PLONKER CREST

12. SPOT THE PLONKER

1. The big match

2. The Wild West

3. Anyone for tennis?

4. At war

5. Mountain climbing

6. Ready, aim . . .

13. THE PLONKER'S GUIDE TO GETTING A GIRL

Even Plonkers get lonely and pine for the opposite sex (that is if a Plonker can be said to *have* an opposite sex). But what are you going to do about it? You won't find the girl of your dreams by hanging around your house on a Saturday night watching *Match of the Day*. No, you've *got* to take the initiative. Here are a few suggestions:

Put an ad in your local newspaper's Lonely Hearts column:

> Boy, 15, spotty, badly dressed, unpopular, boring, poor, without ambition or prospects, seeks beautiful, talented, rich girl, preferably without much taste. In fact, she doesn't have to be beautiful, talented or rich, just alive – sort of.
>
> BOX 007

But I wouldn't expect a lightning response to that one if I were you. While you're waiting, you could:

Take up Ballroom Dancing: Now this can be tricky, especially if you have two – or more – left feet, but it is one sure way of getting within spitting distance (so to speak) of a real, live girl. And the advantage of ballroom dancing, as opposed to the sort of thing they do at school discos, is that you actually get to *hold* the

girl. However, this means that you have to follow some basic rules. For instance:

Do:
1. Wash your hands, especially just after greasing the cat's boils.
2. Leave your ferret at home.
3. Wear socks and – if possible – shoes.

Do not:
1. Wear hobnail boots.
2. Eat a garlic sandwich just before the dance starts.
3. Feel that you must make small-talk with your partner, especially if you have nothing better to say than: "Well, you don't sweat much for a fat girl, do you?"

On the other hand you could:

Answer an ad from your local newsagent's notice board

For instance, you happen to be browsing through the notice board and you see a card:

MS WHIPP

offers disciplinary sessions for naughty boys of all ages. Must be obedient, quiet and obedient. Oh, yes, *and* obedient.
BOX 3003

You *could* write:

> Dear Ms Whipp,
> I saw your card at the newsagent's and wonder if perhaps you might like to be my penpal. My mother says that I am very obedient. And quiet. And obedient.
>
> Yours truly,
>
> A. Plonker (age 15)

But this is *not* likely to result in a long lasting and meaningful relationship. No, by far the most likely place for meeting a suitable girl is at your school. That is, unless you go to an all-boy school.

But, assuming that there *are* girls at your school and you know how to tell them from the boys, *which* of those girls is likely to want to know you?

The short answer to that is: *none* of them.

But don't be discouraged. There are at least ways of finding out whether you have the teensiest chance with the girl of your dreams. For instance, you are walking down the school corridor and you see Donna Lee Snodgrass. Quite naturally, you say: "Er – uh – I mean – uh –" until Donna Lee is well out of earshot.

But let's say you manage to blurt out: "Hello, Donna Lee."

Donna Lee may respond in any one of three ways. She may:

47

1. Throw up
2. Faint
3. Scream for help.

In which case you may have to accept the fact that your chances of making her Donna Lee Plonker are not brilliant. In fact, your chances of getting *any* girl are not brilliant.

You will probably find the following steps compensate for this inadequacy:

1. Whistle loudly at every girl that passes, complimenting the especially attractive ones with "Corrr, look at that fat one move!"
2. Scratch Donna Lee Snodgrass's name on your desk, your glasses, your Dad's car . . .

3. Remember, when you ask a girl to dance with you, "I'd rather have my legs amputated!" means "Yes, please."
4. When meeting your blind date, tell her "Well, you're not quite as ugly as everyone said you'd be."
5. Remember that a girl's aggressiveness, such as hitting you over the head with her handbag and

crying "Leave me alone, you Plonker!" can actually be the first signs of love.

6. Join the priesthood.

14. THE PLONKER BOOK OF BULLIES

Here are some typical bullies a Plonker would be likely to encounter. And how to get your own back . . .

RAYMOND "RATS" RANTZEN: Not strong, but fast. Never hunts in pack of less than four other bullies, which means it is almost impossible to escape. When he has tracked you down, "Rats" likes to sit on your chest while shoving grass up your left nostril. This is not a pleasant experience.
Weakness: a total coward. If two Plonkers stay together, "Rats" and his gang won't dare attack them.

TARQUIN "STYLES" MODISH: Fifth Form prefect, voted "Most Perfectly Dressed" by girls of the Lower Fourth. Doesn't actually bully physically but loves to tease Plonkers about imagined defects in their clothing, such as shouting across schoolyard: "Hey, Plonker! I *do* like your new jumper. What colour is it: snot green or puke brown?"
Weakness: uses hairspray and can't stand the thought that his hair might get messed up. Will retreat at even the thought of a slight breeze. A bucket of water is a good weapon against this particular bully.

NORBERT AND HERBERT HARDWICK: Gigantic fourth-form twins who love to grab a helpless Plonker by his arms and legs and try to pull him apart while shouting "Make a wish, bro!"
Weakness: Can't bear being mistaken for each other. If you always call Norbert "Herbert" and Herbert "Norbert", you might get them to fight each other instead of picking on you.

SIMON BONECRUSHER: The strong est boy in school, can crush a bicep with two fingers of his left hand and loves to demonstrate this useful trick on any Plonker he can catch.
Weakness: totally without brain. Never fails to fall for cry of: "Look out! The head's coming!"

15. THE PLONKER'S SCHOOL NOTEBOOK

a) Egg stain from Plonker's breakfast
b) Tyre tracks from being thrown under bus (while still in Plonker's pocket) by Simon Bonecrusher
c) Grease spot from school cafeteria chips
d) Marks made when Sis couldn't find anything else to blot her lipstick
e) Plonker's address, including: "Planet Earth, the Universe, the Cosmos, the . . . (stopped when he couldn't think of anything bigger)
f) Blood from when the Plonker stabbed himself with his biro
g) Name of Subject
h) Addition by class wit
i) Name of Plonker's secret ideal woman and love object "Donna Lee" (crossed out when Donna Lee saw it)
j) Teacher's comment
k) Caricature of headmaster (not by Plonker, but he got the blame, anyway)
l) Another addition by class wit
m) Rude comment by anonymous source
n) Inside: totally blank

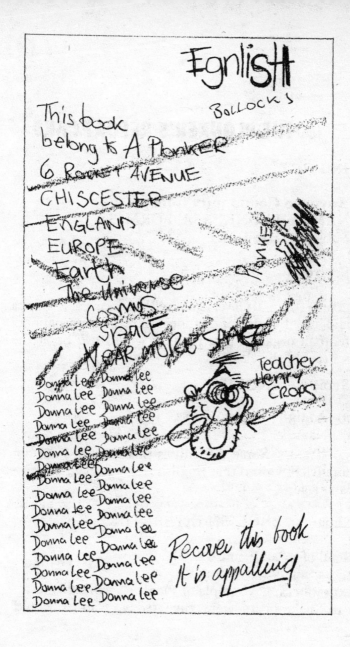

Egnlish

Bollocks

This book
belong to A Plonker
6 Rocket Avenue
CHISCESTER
ENGLAND
EUROPE
Earth
The Universe
Cosmus
SPACE
A BAR MORE SPACE

Ronnie is A wanker

Donna Lee Donna Lee
Donna Lee Donna Lee
Donna Lee Donna Lee
Donna Lee Donna Lee
Donna Lee Donna Lee
Donna Lee Donna Lee
Donna Lee Donna Lee
Donna Lee Donna Lee
Donna Lee Donna Lee
Donna Lee Donna Lee
Donna Lee Donna Lee
Donna Lee Donna Lee
Donna Lee Donna Lee
Donna Lee Donna Lee
Donna Lee Donna Lee

Teacher
Henry
CROPS

Recover this book
It is appalling

16. THE PLONKER'S REPORT CARD

REPORT

Anytown Community College
NAME: PLONKER, A. FORM..3.6
Subject: HISTORY

Set 0 of 8   Exam: 0.8%

COMMENTS: If Oliver Cromwell had discovered America and the League of Nations were an international football organization, Plonker would *still* be at the bottom of the class.

Subject: ENGLISH

Set 0 of 8   Exam: –2%

COMMENTS: Some difficulties this term as I am not totally convinced that English *is* this student's native language.

Subject: ENGLISH LITERATURE

Set 0 of 8   Exam: 9%

COMMENTS: A sample of Plonker's work this term: "If Shakespeare were alive today, Hamlet would probably be playing in defence for West Bromwich Albion." Need I say more?

Subject: CHEMISTRY

Set 0 of 8   Exam: 4.5%

COMMENTS: Accidentally created $CH_2NO_3CHNO_3CH_2NO_3$ (nitroglycerin) and blew up college labs (twice). To sum up the potential of this student, I can only say: HELP !!!!!!!!

Subject: RELIGIOUS EDUCATION

Set 0 of 8   Exam: 18%

COMMENTS: Plonker is a quiet, orderly student. In fact, we were eight weeks into the term before I was able to discover that he thinks that the established religion of Great Britain is tree worship. I am beginning to wonder myself.

Subject: GEOGRAPHY

Set 0 of 8   Exam: 2%

COMMENTS: Thanks to Plonker's unique contributions to the class, half of the students think that Europe is an island in the middle of the largest lake in Tibet and that Vladivostok is the name of a small foreign car. The other half are *sure* of it.

Subject: FRENCH

Set 0 of 8   Exam: don't ask

COMMENTS: While on class trip to Calais, I asked Plonker to enquire of a policeman the way to the railway station. I'm still not sure exactly what he said but we were all arrested immediately for espionage, black mail and insulting the honour of France. Next year I'm teaching German.

Subject: MUSIC

Set 0 of 8   Exam: not measurable

COMMENTS: Plonker has attempted six different instruments this term and has somehow made them all sound like tissue paper and comb. *Very* badly played tissue paper and comb.

Subject: PHYSICAL EDUCATION

Set 0 of 8   Exam: 0%

COMMENTS: Plonker is a difficult student to assess. He is so dangerous around *any* kind of athletic equipment that he spends every class in the laundry hamper. He has *still* managed to seriously injure half of the class.

Subject: MATHEMATICS

Set 0 of 8   Exam: less than zero

COMMENTS: When Plonker came into my class I was
certain that 2+2=4. Now I'm not so sure.

REPORT   Date: 20/12/89
Times Absent: not often enough
Times Late: 60 out of 60

Some of Plonker's teachers this term would like to see
him expelled from school and, if possible, deported
from the country. The others disagree. They don't

think this would be harsh enough. Personally, I talked to Plonker only once this term and that was one too many times. Please accept this as my resignation from teaching.*

* This report has had to be dictated due to the fact that I am in a straitjacket.

HEAD OF FORM
REPORT

If I hear the name Plonker again this year, I'll scream. In fact, I think I'll scream, anyway. YAAAAAA-RGGGHHHHHH!!! HEAD OF YEAR

REPORT

Plonker? I can't recall any Plonker at this College. HEADMASTER

17. THE PLONKER'S ALIBI

What to say when a teacher points his bony finger at you and says: "Gotcha!":

For instance: when the Deputy Head accuses you of some terrible deed – say supergluing the school cat's tail to the portrait of the school founder in the school corridor so that it looks like he has a moustache – and rounds up some of the school's most likely villains, including, of course, you, a Plonker.

FOUNDER

DEPUTY HEAD: Ridley, did you do it?

RIDLEY: No, sir. It couldn't have been me because my Auntie Vi's third cousin Elmo was visiting us yesterday and I had to stay home to grease the parrot's feet.

DEPUTY HEAD: Right, off you go then. How about you, Whitelaw?

WHITELAW: No, sir. I was excused gym on Wednesday and the headmaster asked me to scrape rust off of the school cannon.

DEPUTY HEAD: That eliminates you, I suppose. What's your excuse, Lawson?

LAWSON: I couldn't have done it, sir. That was the day that Daphne Hogan brought her pet angora rabbit to school and it escaped. Hurd and I chased it across the street and it was run over by a busload of tourists from Yugoslavia. You never saw such a mess in your life, sir, honestly!

DEPUTY HEAD: (with sigh) All right, all right. Now hurry or you'll be late for class.

Lawson scampers off and Deputy Head fixes *you* with beady eye.

DEPUTY HEAD: You – Thingiewhatsit – (it is a true fact that teachers can almost never remember a Plonker's name) I suppose *you've* got an excuse, too?

PLONKER: Me, sir? Just because my fingers are stuck together with superglue? The school cat never did like me, you know. And those long grey hairs on my jacket are just . . .

DEPUTY HEAD: You did it! Write ten thousand lines every day after school for the next million years.

MORAL: You might as well be guilty. They'll never believe you, anyway.

18. THE COUNTRY DIARY OF AN EDWARDIAN PLONKER

June 1906

The badge of June is green of hue
And if you're not very careful
You'll get your nostrils stuffed
With grass.*

                       Local folk legend

3rd Went with Professor Pucklemeyer's class on a nature ramble. I volunteered to carry the compass. Unfortunately, I slightly misread the directions, and we got lost. Rescued three days later by West Shrumpshire Constabulary and Mountain Rescue Patrol half way up Mount Dimple.

7th Great excitement. A pair of lesser spotted Twirtwistles, thought to be extinct since early in the reign of Victoria, were reported in Cholmondley Woods, and Prof Pucklemeyer took a group of us out to see if we could find their nest and perhaps some eggs. After a long, hot ramble, we stopped and sat down to rest. When we got up, I went to brush off the tails of my coat and discovered that I'd been sitting on the elusive Twirtwistle nest – with eggs. Prof Pucklemeyer punched me in the arm. Cost of having coat cleaned: 5 shillings, 6 pence.

11th Again out with Professor Pucklemeyer's class on a botany ramble. This time, Haverstraw took over the compass, but I was allowed to carry the packed lunches. Somehow I dropped them in a stream. The professor was not pleased. Haverstraw punched me in the arm. V. Painful.

22nd   Somehow I missed hearing about the nature ramble, but came across Professor Pucklemeyer and the others on the other side of Badger Brook. I hallooed them, but perhaps the wind blew my voice away because I had to really hurry to catch them up. The professor apologized for hitting me in the arm and said that they were looking for a very rare species of wild violet (*v. hardtofindensus*), and wouldn't I like to go skip stones in the brook or something. Instead, I offered to join their search, and Prof Pucklemeyer agreed, though he must have been feeling rather sad, for he sighed so loudly. He stressed that if I found the rare violet I must let him know *immediately*. As luck would have it, no more than five minutes later I spotted the very flower we were looking for and hurried to the professor's side, shouting: "I've found it!"

"Where?" he cried excitedly.

"Here!" I said, holding the clump of violets out at arm's length for him to see.

27th   No nature ramble as Professor Pucklemeyer has had to go away for a long rest. Liniment for sore arm: 3 shillings, 4 pence.

*Too true.

19. THE PLONKER'S HOROSCOPE

AQUARIUS (The Wet One) 21 January–19 February
Today be sure to look out for bullies bearing buckets
of water. Whoops! Too late. Now go home and
change your clothes.

PISCES (Fishface) 20 February–20 March
You will eat a tuna sandwich and get food poisoning.
No, there's no use arguing. It is written in your stars.
You might as well open your lunch box and get on
with it. The one on stale white bread with cabbage
leaves.

ARIES (The Scapegoat) 21 March–20 April
You will be blamed for everything that happens this
week, including an earthquake in Peru, so you might
as well just get used to it. Hard cheese.

TAURUS (The Bullshooter) 21 April–21 May
You'd better have your best lies available today because you will need them.

GEMINI (The Cricket) 22 May–21 June
Stay away from net practice today or you'll end up wearing a cricket ball in your left ear.

CANCER (The Crabby One) 22 June–23 July
This will be a good week to avoid getting within several square kilometres of the Deputy Headmaster. A change of continents – or planets – would be a good idea.

LEO (The Roarer) 24 July–23 August
Definitely not a great day to stick your head in a lion's mouth. Or go to school, for that matter. Spend the day in bed. Or under it.

VIRGO (The Shy One) 24 August–23 September
The girl of your dreams will notice you today. In fact, she'll accuse you of stealing her lunch money. Might as well confess. They won't believe you anyway.

LIBRA (The Loser) 24 September–23 October
You will have a close escape from the school bully today by dodging into the boys' toilets. Unfortunately, that's where you will blunder into the weekly meeting of the school's Society for Human Sacrifice.

SCORPIO (The Bitten One) 24 October–22 November
Your school will have an infestation of lice and guess
who gets the blame. Right.

SAGITTARIUS (The Target) 23 November–21 December
Whatever you do, do *not* accept an invitation to join
the school's archery team at practice today. Purchase
a chain-mail jumper on the way to school just in case.

CAPRICORN (The *Other* Scapegoat) 22 December–
20 January
Improve your popularity by practising useful phrases:
"It's a fair cop." "I confess, sir, I did it." "I don't
know what came over me."

20. LEAVES FROM A PLONKER'S BOOK OF POETRY

Into the Valley of Death

Into the Valley of Death
Rode the valiant 400 Plonkers
Came a cry from those standing by:
By Gad, they must be bonkers!

The Plonker Stood on the Burning Deck

The Plonker stood on the burning deck
His ship was sinking fast,
Her prow was under water
The night she could not last.

Sometimes I think, he mused, more with rue than ire
It might not have been so very smart to start that little
    fire.

I Had a Little Fruit Tree

I had a little fruit tree
Nothing would it bear
But golden apples and diamond pears
My, how the Plonkers did gather to stare.

I cut it down, naturally.

How Do I Love Thee, Plonker Mine?

How do I love thee, Plonker mine?
Let me count the ways.

First there's . . . on the other hand . . .
Could you come back in a couple of days?

Barefoot Boy with Cheek of Tan

Barefoot boy with cheek of tan
What will you be when you're a man?

A farmer or a sailor, a cowboy or a tailor?
A seamster who sews, a teacher who knows?
A tinker or a thief, a lawyer with a brief?
Or a general who leads armies to conquer?

Oh, I care not what's my lot,
I'll sweep floors or open doors,
I'll preach from the bible or sue for libel
As long as I'm not a Plonker.

Plonker, Plonker Quite Contrary

Plonker, Plonker quite contrary
How does your garden grow?
With thistles here and twitch grass there
And nettles all in a row

I Shot an Arrow Into the Air

I shot an arrow into the air
Thank goodness for the National Health Service

The Village Plonker

Under the spreading chestnut tree
The village Plonker stood
Shoeing horses, mending pots
Doing naught but good.
So, why the frown upon the Plonker's face,
As he tends to the ploughman's brute?
Is he thinking, perhaps, about the fact
That the horse is standing on his foot?

21. PLONKERS IN HISTORY

WILLIAM THE PLONQUERER: Norman fishmonger's apprentice who was supposed to invade Britain in 1066 with Duke William but overslept.

SIR GUY PLONKERVILLE: Scion of old West Country family, owner of the spooky Plonkerville Hall and famed as the breeder of the fearsome and ferocious Hound of the Plonkervilles which was said to bay on the moors whenever a Plonkerville was in serious trouble. In this particular case, it was because Sir Guy forgot the Doggie Munchies one dark and stormy night when he went out to feed the Hound.

DAVY PLONKER: One of the most famous guides and trappers on the American frontier who unfortunately got lost and starved to death one day when he was trying to find his way from Sam's Barbershop to Bojangles Good Eats Café in old New Orleans.

HANS VAN PLONKERER: The little Dutch boy who was working in his father's tulip fields one day when he noticed that a tiny leak had started in a dike. Aware that the leak had to be stopped instantly or the entire village would be drowned by the icy waters of the north Sea, Hans quickly tried to plug the tiny hole in the dike by sticking an ice lolly in it. Unfortunately, this did not work very well.

BILLY THE PLONKER: Youngest, fastest gun in old Tombstone, Arizona. Unfortunately, also the worst shot. In the famous "Shoot-out at the K.O. Corral" against Doc Holiday, two of the three Earp brothers and Miss Suzee of the Comb 'n' Snip beauty boutique, Billy missed all of them and managed to shoot himself in the foot, hip, elbow and left earlobe. Retired from gunslinging early to work at an automatic covered wagon wash.

THE SCARLET PLONKERNEL: "They seek him here . . . they seek him there . . ." Unfortunately for the Scarlet Plonkernel, scourge of the French Revolution who rescued many a Royalist from the Guillotine, they also *found* him here and there when the Scarlet Plonkernel accidentally dropped his bus pass revealing his name *and* address.

22. PLONKERS IN SPORT

FOOTBALL: Benny "Shell-shocked" Carter, most scored upon goalkeeper in the history of football. Record: Goals against: 9,999 (excluding 99 own goals by Benny himself).

AMERICAN FOOTBALL: Rodney "The Cooker" Rodney, quarterback for Poughkipsie Peewitts, mistook centre's head for football and threw it 60 yards for the team's only touchdown of the year. Disallowed.

ANCIENT OLYMPICS: Gaius Plonkus (42–15 BC) entered both marathon and hammer throw but came in last because he did not realize that he did not have to carry the hammer on the 26-mile run.

MODERN OLYMPICS: Tarquin Tartan won Britain's first Olympic gold medal since 1950 when squat tag was accepted as an official Olympic event.

WATER POLO: Hon Danby Smythe-Smith-Smythe nearly won a place on the British team for the Commonwealth Games, but was disqualified when his horse drowned.

CABER TOSSING: Hamish MacPlonker mistook a telephone pole for his caber and knocked out communications for two counties.

CRICKET: L.B.W. "Ducks" Cromarty, twelfth man for minor county of Shrimphamptonshire, renowned for not having scored a single run in fifteen seasons.

RUGBY: Zeke "Kamekazi" Figby, picked up a dropped ball and disappeared under the pack of the New Malden Maulers never to be seen again.

23. PLONKERS IN INDUSTRY

SID WURZEL: Automobile plant worker who set a new world's record by assembling, single-handed, a .1 litre Sparrowfart Turbo thruster hatchback convertible in only 29 minutes.

MICK THISTLETWAITE: Elected to Office Boy Hall of Fame for his feat of making every single delivery of post to the wrong employee of MegaBucks International for an entire year, cinching his place by delivering notice of bankruptcy papers to the company's retired tea lady.

REX FINKNOTTLE: Celebrated dogbreeder who crossed a ferocious pitbull mastiff with a greyhound and has been running ever since.

SIR VIVIAN BRATWURST, O.B.E.: War-time industrialist whose factory – working day and night – finally completed a consignment of ten thousand Thunderflash fighter planes for the British government the day *after* the war ended. Sir Vivian had very little luck convincing the public that these planes, suitably modified, made the perfect runabout for shopping in town.

IVOR BIGBRAIN: Chief scientist for Global Whatsit plc, responsible for inventing automatic windows and windscren wipers for submarines.

24. PLONKERS IN SCIENCE

CHEMISTRY: Ephram Marphe, Ph.D.
Was performing an experiment demonstrating the creation of hydrogen gas when laboratory lights went out. Lit match.

NUCLEAR SCIENCE: Eli Whynney, M.Sc.
Discovered a new way to split the atom by placing the atom on a concrete slab and hitting it with his forehead.

BIOTECHNOLOGY: Dr I.Q. Zero
Discovered the technology required to create an animal with the brain of a flea, the speed of a sloth, the courage of a newt, the imagination of a clam and the grace of a slug (*Plonkerus Plonkerus*), but nobody could think of a use for such a creature.

ANATOMY: Professor Y. Ignatz
Attempted to demonstrate to his class how to dissect a medium-sized mammal, namely a mountain lion. The mountain lion was only sleeping.

BOTANY: Melvin M. Melvin
While out mountain climbing discovered very rare species of plant. Reached out to pick it. With both hands.

25. PLONKERS IN POLITICS AND GOVERNMENT

GERALD FUNK, M.P.: Member for West Loathing since 1958 was known as "The Silent Man of the House" because he sat there day in and day out without saying a single word. This was mistaken for reserve and wisdom until 1983 when it was discovered that Mr Funk had been dead since 1962.

LORD BRUTE OF BRUTELY: Backwoods peer who lives so far out in the country that it is in a different time zone from London. Several times a year he is captured, caged and delivered to the House of Lords to vote the Government line on a bill which might be defeated. Doesn't actually speak any known language, but this is unnecessary as all he has to do is listen for the division bell and then get up and shamble toward the appropriate lobby – that is, the one where the Government left the lumps of raw meat.

GENERAL SIR LLEWELLYN LAGGARDLY, BT: Exalted High Commander of the Doorknocker of the House of Lords whose only job is to knock once a year on the door of the House of Commons, upon which signal the entire House cries out: "Go away, you Plonker!" and he does and isn't seen again until the same time the next year.

RT. HON VYVIAN FISHPASTE-SMELLIE, CBE: Shadow Minister for Belly Button Lint who periodically rises in the House to demand what the Government's Minister for Belly Button Lint is doing about the overwhelming glut and/or alarming scarcity of that strategically vital substance on which Britain's place among the great nations of the world depends.

HON JERMAYNE BLATHERTH WAITE: Inherited the family seat for East Hugger in 1851 but didn't actually get around to attending the House of Commons until, in 1889, he just happened to be passing Parliament Square and dropped in out of curiosity. Was so shocked by his fellow MPs that he went to bed with his hat on and stayed there for the rest of his life.

PEREGRIN PEW, O.B.E.: Consul General of Asphasia, Central Africa, went home on leave to London in 1899 and on returning couldn't quite remember where Asphasia was, exactly. Was appointed Ambassador-at-large and spent twenty years wandering around the Dark Continent without ever finding the missing country. Pew became known as "the man who lost the British Empire, or at least a small part of it."

THE FAIRLY HONOURABLE J. SHIFTLESS BASKET, MEP (Member of the European Parliament): Chief lifeguard of the Common Market Milk Lake. Salary: £75,000 a year. Basket's only qualification for this important position is that he can't swim.

26. PLONKERS IN OUTER SPACE

COL. YURI WANDERDOFF: Russian Cosmonaut who took part in a space walk without first connecting the cable which should have attached him to the spaceship.

BBWXTL ZNERRRRK: First space traveller from planet Og from a spiral nebulae on the other side of Uranus. Unfortunately, he made a landing on the planet Earth without realizing that the shape and size of his space ship could be a bit of a problem.

GUS GROMLEY: Janitor at Cape Kennedy Space Center, Florida, who hadn't finished mopping out interior of *Serendipity Seven* space rocket when the count-down started. Currently sweeping up the dark side of the smallest moon of Jupiter.

TARQUIN SMYTHE-BOTTOMLY: Nearly first Briton in Outer Space, but caused last-second cancellation of multi-million pound mission when he suddenly remembered that he'd forgotton his biro.

PRINCE PLONXXX: Youngest son of Emperor Zartak the Rude, lord of the northwestern segment of the universe. Appointed governor of smallest moon of Planet Janet, but his mighty army of highly trained and heavily armed interstellar stormtroopers was defeated by a squadron of alien budgies. Now assistant cloakroom attendant on a planet the size of a Skoda fastback.

27. SEVEN DANGEROUS SIGNS THAT YOU MAY BE CEASING TO BE A PLONKER

Watch out for these symptoms which can warn you of the danger that you are ceasing to be a Plonker. Turn to the Plonker's Credo (page 37) to attempt a cure.

1.   The distance between your cuff and the top of your shoe shrinks to less than five inches.

2.   Your teacher actually remembers your name.

3. The school bully goes three days in a row without hitting you.

4. Someone else is chosen to appear on the DO *NOT* COME TO SCHOOL LOOKING LIKE THIS side of the School Dress Code poster.

5. You do not spill soup, tea, coffee, blood or radioactive cobalt 17 on your tie for a whole day.

6. You catch (rather than fall under) the school bus.

7. Somebody else gets the blame.

28. ARE *YOU* A PLONKER? TEST

Have you ever wondered: "Could *I* possibly be a Plonker?" If the answer to that question has cost you any sleep, just complete the following test and set your mind at ease. Or something.

1. Some toughs are tormenting a lame dog in the street. Do you:

  A) Try to stop them and get beaten up.
  B) Do nothing and get arrested along with them for cruelty to animals.
  C) Wait until they leave to try to help the dog and get badly bitten.

2. Donna Lee Snodgrass drops her books in the corridor as you are walking behind her. Do you:

   A) Trip over them.
   B) Try to stop others stepping on them and get trampled yourself.
   C) Pick them up and get accused of trying to steal Donna's books.

3. Someone has stolen all of the money collected for the class's coach trip to the Sellafield Nuclear Reactor. Do you:

A) Come to school wearing all of your Ban-the-Bomb buttons.

B) Pull out your handkerchief and spill £30.89 worth of small change on the floor.

C) Accidentally burn your hands ironing a shirt so that you are the only member of the class who can't be fingerprinted.

4. There is only one sausage left in the cafeteria at lunchtime: Do you:

A) Take it and get food poisoning.

B) Offer it to the next person in line (Simon Bonecrusher) and get the sausage shoved up your nose.

C) Start to take it, change your mind, put it back, take it again and get sent to the Deputy Head for mucking about with food in the cafeteria.

5. Your teacher asks for a volunteer to take a message to the Headmaster's office. Do you:

A) Do nothing and get in teacher's bad books for lack of cooperation.

B) Volunteer and get jeered at for being teacher's pet.

C) Raise your hand and say that ordinarily you would be only too pleased to do this but you've got a sore foot because your Uncle Ernie dropped a red-hot bowling ball on it.

6. The school bully is sitting on your chest in the schoolyard when "God Save the Queen" is played over the Tannoy. Do you:

A) Struggle to rise to your feet and get thumped for your efforts.
B) Just lie there and get reported for lack of patriotism.
C) Lie there at attention while humming along with the music.

SCORING: For every A answer give yourself 5 points
For every B answer give yourself 3 points For every C answer give yourself 1 point

RESULTS: 1-7 points: You are very possibly a Plonker
8-20 points: You are probably a Plonker
20+ points: If *you're* not a Plonker, who is?